Fireflies

Fireflies

Memory, Identity, and Poetry

David P. Owen, Jr.

SENSE PUBLISHERS
ROTTERDAM/BOSTON/TAIPEI

A C.I.P. record for this book is available from the Library of Congress.

ISBN: 978-94-6351-147-6 (paperback)
ISBN: 978-94-6351-148-3 (hardback)
ISBN: 978-94-6351-149-0 (e-book)

Published by: Sense Publishers,
P.O. Box 21858,
3001 AW Rotterdam,
The Netherlands
https://www.sensepublishers.com/

Cover image: "Left Behind" by Courtney Rae Hancock Owen

Printed on acid-free paper

For Courtney and Patrick, the two best poems I know

TABLE OF CONTENTS

TABLE OF CONTENTS

ACKNOWLEDGMENTS

I first want to thank God for a world full of mystery and wonder and beauty, even if we don't always see it. I would also like to thank all of the family and friends who find parts of their own lives in these pages, and Mary Aswell Doll, Matt Gramling, Sheila Hancock, Jason Harwell, Drew Lawson, Carl Leggo, William M. Reynolds, and John A. Weaver for their advice and encouragement about this project. Finally, I want to thank the hundreds of students over the years whose poetry experiments have helped me form these ideas.

The following poems appear in a different context in *The Need for* Revision: *Curriculum, Literature, and the 21st Century* (2011), and I thank Sense Publishers for allowing them to be part of this work as well: "Each morning is a gift," "Forsythia," "Phaethon," "Humidity," "Resurrection," "Procrastination," "Love and Hate," "Vacation Bible School," "A Short Interview about Poetry," "Memory," "Smoke," and "What it Meant."

SONGS OF OURSELVES

Why We Should All Be Poets

1

This is a book of memory, identity, and poetry—and also a book *about* memory, identity, and poetry. It is also a book about writing books—a book written in the hopes that other books will be written. Maybe by you.

2

Poets are the unacknowledged legislators of the World. (Percy Shelley, 1840/1977)

Poetry is dead. Does anybody really care? (Bruce Wexler, 2003)

To live is to read texts, but to be alive is to write them. (Alan A. Block, 1988/1999)

The question, O me! So sad, recurring—What good amid
these, O me, O life?
               Answer.
That you are here—that life exists and identity,
That the powerful play goes on, and you may contribute a verse. (Walt Whitman, 1892/1993)

When Percy Shelley said poets were the "unacknowledged legislators of the World" (1840/1977) in his *Defence of Poetry*, poets were rock stars. Or at least that's how they seemed in high school literature class (in this case courtesy of *McDougal Littell Literature: British Literature*, 2011). Shelley embraced radical politics (p. 846), William Blake had prophetic visions (p. 752), and Samuel Taylor Coleridge was a philosopher/opium addict (p. 796/p. 825). William Wordsworth was a proto-hippie (p. 782) wandering the Lake District, John Keats died young and then got famous (p. 860), and Lord Byron was, well, Lord Byron, inventor of most of the rock star clichés you can think of (p. 832). Later, Robert Browning had fanatical followers (p. 924), T.S. Eliot called the world a Waste Land (p. 1092), and Dylan Thomas gave passionate, emotional performances and had a massive drinking problem (p. 1158). Sure, there were poets who were no doubt quiet, upstanding members of their communities and devoted family men, but they seemed like the exception rather than the rule; poets, for a long time, were "solitary figures engaged in a long, and sometimes elusive, quest; often they were also social nonconformists or outcasts" (Abrams, 1999, p. 179). They were pioneers and visionaries, unique and powerful voices of a generation endowed with a special sensitivity to the world and a heightened gift for "the very image of life expressed in its eternal truth" (Shelley, 1840/1977, p. 485).

This "rock star" impression holds pretty well until and through the time of actual rock stars; the famous music film/goodbye concert of The Band, *The Last Waltz* (1978), is a "who's who" of rock and roll royalty, but it also features readings by Michael McClure and Lawrence Ferlinghetti. And some of those rock stars were actually occasionally called poets; in fact, not only can you still find Bob Dylan, Patti Smith, and Leonard Cohen in poetry anthologies, here and there, but Dylan has just been honored with a Nobel Prize in Literature. Even today, you could make the case that poets enjoy a special esteem in our culture; we still name a U.S. Poet Laureate every few years, and while musicians and football teams get invited to the White House on a pretty regular basis, when it's time to inaugurate a new President, we sometimes bring in a poet for the ceremony.

3

However, in some ways even rock stars don't seem to be rock stars anymore, diminished by factors like slowing sales and the absence of a cultural mainstream, and not everyone these days thinks that writing poetry, or even reading it, is a good use of anyone's time. These people, and there are lots of them, and many that I would call friends, usually say the kinds of things that Bruce Wexler does in his article for *Newsweek* entitled "Poetry is Dead. Does Anybody Really Care?" (2003). Since I first read this article, I have used it countless times with my students in order to have just this discussion about what poetry is, and has been, and will be in the future. Wexler, like many of us, "can no longer even name a living poet," even though he claims to have once loved Lowell and Berryman. He says he "hated the poetry unit in English class," with its "rhymed and rhythmic writing" and "tangled symbol and allusion," and complains that he always wondered why poets "couldn't just say what they meant." And though he claims that at some point in college, he "got it," he also reports that he soon "got married, had children, pursued [his] career, bought a house," and eventually "found more relevance in articles about interest rates." Many of my students agree with these sentiments, and even some of those who like poetry, or are at least sympathetic to its plight (or mine), agree with Wexler that today "people don't possess the patience to read a poem 20 times before the sound and sense of it takes hold."

These conversations with my students are hard for me, even if I think they are important to have. I try to get them to see how Seamus Heaney told us we could "dig" for ourselves with poetry (1998), how Walt Whitman encouraged us to find the "open road" (1892/1993). I show them how Langston Hughes used poetry to mine a difficult background in "Cross" (1926/2002), and how Sharon Olds said we should use our own voices in "Take the 'I' Out" (1999). I point out that poets are often trying to say things that can't be said—at least easily—and so they *are* trying to say what they mean. I even try to get them to explore the ways in which hip hop and other popular musical forms keep alive an attention to wordplay and poetic techniques. A lot of my students, though—at least at first—agree with part, or much, of what Wexler says about poetry's death. And though I think they are wrong about poetry—enough to write a book about it, even—I understand where they are coming from, and why they feel the way they do. After all, even though poets seem to have been rock stars in Shelley's day, they still had their detractors, even then; it is worth noting that Shelley felt the need to write a "Defence," of course, and Raymond Williams points out that "the last pages of Shelley's *Defence of Poetry* are painful to read" (1962/1970). As he puts it, Shelley can say that poets are the "unacknowledged legislators of the world" (1840/1977), but the description of them as "unacknowledged" unfortunately "carries with it also the helplessness of a generation" (Williams, 1962/1970, p. 285). Writers in Shelley's day were trying to learn to trade a "system of patronage" for the "general commercial publishing of the modern kind" (p. 272), and that new reading public seemed to increasingly want the same kind of practical relevance that Wexler describes. High school literature books may make poets, especially the Romantic ones, sound like rock stars, but even if our impression is accurate, it is also likely that they were the kind of rock stars who had to endure growing criticism and pressures from people like the drunken friend in the famous poem "Terence, this is stupid stuff" by A. E. Housman (1896/1993, line 14): "Come, pipe a tune to dance to, lad."

4

And when I was my students' age, I have to admit that I would likely have agreed with Wexler, and maybe even that famous friend of Terence, on many points as well. I liked poetry well enough, at least as a diversion from the math and science studies I thought were more practical, and serious, and useful. But I didn't read much poetry, and I never wrote any. I was a big reader of fiction, but I had very little arts education growing up, and most of my free time was filled with sports. I don't think these things were bad necessarily, but they don't really lay a good foundation for a love of poetry at a young age. Even when I did decide to try my hand at creative writing, I chose songwriting; I wanted to learn to play the guitar, I enjoyed singing, and I'm sure I would have told you then how much more relevant it was, or at least more fun.

But then I became a literature major in college, and found myself reading, and liking, a lot more poetry. And a few years later, when I began teaching literature and writing classes, I found myself assigning students to write poetry as well. About the same time, I began to write some of my own poems. And when I went back to graduate school, this time in curriculum studies, I went with a new appreciation for poetry, and it seemed that everywhere I looked there were theorists ready to tell me why I had changed my mind. Here was Alfred Hofstadter, explaining that for Heidegger, "at the basis of man's ability to build in the sense of cultivating and constructing there must be, as a primal source, his poetic ability, the ability to take the measure of the world" (1971, xiv); there was Hegel, arguing that "poetry is the universal art of the mind which has become free in its own nature" (1886/1993). By the time I got the chance to write my first book, *The Need for* Revision: *Curriculum, Literature, and the 21st Century* (2011), I had become convinced that the world, and certainly the public school curriculum, needs more poetry in it. I argued for the study of poetry as well as for living and working more poetically in the broader sense, in a variety of fields, and pointed out that literature courses for high school students are the ideal places for these approaches to take hold. In the second chapter, I dealt particularly with poetry, and even wrote both *in* poetry and about it.

What I had discovered is that studying poetry, and especially *writing* poetry, is good for us, for me, for my students, in so many ways. It lets us express ourselves free of the prison of social language convention; it lets us explore complexities, and subtleties, and details everywhere that so often go unnoticed in the rush of the day-to-day; it lets us swim in the rich, full, turbulent sea of metaphor; it lets us live free of the answer key. As Sandra L. Faulkner puts it, we can "say things in poetic lines that can't be stated in other ways" (2014, p. xxvi). It is also perhaps, because of these qualities, the best way to experience autobiography and *currere* as theorists like Pinar and Grumet explain them. Grumet says that in autobiography, "the writer can turn back upon her own texts and see there her own processes and biases of selection at work. It is there that curriculum as thought is revealed as the screen through which we pass curriculum as lived" (1980/1999, p. 25). She also says that "I organize my story as I organize my world, and it is my story of the past that can tell me where I am and where I am going" (p. 27). Pinar says of his "method of *currere*" that it is "regressive—progressive—analytical—synthetical" and hopes to "explore the complex relation between the temporal and conceptual" in order to "disclose their relation to the Self and its evolution and education" (1975/1994); the recollection of details from our past and articulation of our hopes for the future seem like ideal material for poetry. I had discovered, in short, that poetry isn't really some mystical ability that blesses a select few; poetry is something you *do*, a way of living and approaching life that enriches it, no "rock star" context required.

5

In fact, maybe this "rock star" impression isn't good for us, or for poetry, at all. First of all, as many have noted, the poets we study in school are overwhelmingly old, white men. And while that might be historically accurate for a British Literature textbook, at least in terms of fame and influence (or maybe *access* to fame and influence), it is hardly representative of or relatable to the variety of students studying literature in our classrooms today. Secondly, even if we ignore race and gender and culture, the same visionary, blessed, powerful uniqueness that makes our rock star poets so impressive also makes them distant and untouchable; over and over again, we are reminded that *they* are not *us*. And anyway, it almost always isn't even true; lots of great poets were pretty regular people as well. The same McDougal-Littell text that gives us so many juicy details about the Romantics also tells us that Matthew Arnold was a school inspector (2011, p. 1034), and Adam Kirsh reminds us that "William Carlos Williams was a family doctor," and that "T.S. Eliot was a banker when he wrote 'The Waste Land'" (2016). Maybe we have it backwards, and Lord Byron is not the model but the exception. I wonder if this "rock star" idea about poets also led, strangely, to what at least seems like Wexler's most damaging criticism of contemporary poetry: "poetry is the only art form where the number of people creating it is far greater than the number of people appreciating it" (2003). In other words, poets are rock stars with no fans. Ouch. But wait—can that even possibly be true? Wexler makes it sound like there are people out there who write poetry but somehow don't like it. Surely that can't be what he means. Is he saying, instead, that the number of people who write poetry is greater than the number of people who like poetry but don't write it? Here Wexler seems to be imagining a distant, admiring audience that used to exist but doesn't anymore.

Who are those people, the ones who love poetry but don't write any? And if they ever existed in large numbers, wouldn't that be highly unusual? Wexler seems to argue that something is only lively and successful if it has throngs of fans who don't participate in the action. Such a situation in any art, or field of interest, or form of entertainment, is pretty hard to imagine: scores of baseball fans who never picked up a bat or wore a glove, crowds of people who love to hear stories but don't tell any themselves, music nuts everywhere who never started a band in their garage. Sure, only some poets become "pros," but the same is true in football, and no one thinks it's dying. The very opposite of Wexler's point seems to be more likely, all over the place, and certainly in poetry: we participate in the things we love, and that love grows with the participation. Do we really think baseball is dying if the kids who watch it sign up for little league? If adults join softball leagues? If music fans start bands or sing karaoke—or just in the shower—does that mean popular music is in trouble as an art form? I would argue instead that poetry is the kind of thing that comes to life the more you participate in it; perhaps the best way to "get" poetry, and maybe to come to love it, is to write it as well as read it.

And the more we participate in poetry, the more good it does us—the more we "get" ourselves, too. Sandra L. Faulkner (2014), for one, likes that "poetry is a conversation between my personas, a recognition of how identities are multiple, fluid and sometimes contentious" (p. xv). Carl Leggo (2012), as well, supports "a poetics of research by investigating ways that creative writing contributes to knowing and understanding" (p. xiii). In fact, there are many poets who seem to think of poetry in this way, and when I first encountered the ideas of Grumet and Pinar, I couldn't help but think of Robert Penn Warren. Warren is maybe the most famous poet no one's heard of; he's won seemingly every award a writer could hope for, including a Pulitzer for both prose and poetry, and yet I didn't encounter his work until graduate school, and still get confused looks when I cite him as one of my favorites. When I did finally find his poetry, though, I was hooked for good, and found myself

5

reading again and again the handful of (poorly) Xeroxed copies of Warren's late works, which I eventually traded for his *Collected Poems* (1998); in the foreword to that text, Harold Bloom says it is an "American masterwork" and that between the "ages of sixty-one and eighty-one, [Warren] had enjoyed a poetic renascence fully comparable to the great final phases of Thomas Hardy, William Butler Yeats, and Wallace Stevens" (1998). No one has made me want to write poetry more than Warren, and I was struck particularly by the way Warren turned again and again to the subjects of time, memory, and identity in his late work. He seemed to be doing in those poems much what Grumet and Pinar say we all should do.

6

James Dickey once described Robert Penn Warren's considerable body of work as "a long, lyric, and dramatic meditation on time" (1984, p. 81), and one does not have to look deeply into Warren's poetry for evidence of this statement. The concept of time seems almost to play the role of an allegorical character in much of Warren's poetry; Dickey even goes so far as to say that "the excruciating mystery of being, and being in time ... *is* Warren, and has been with him always" (p. 88). Countless critics have written countless articles and books that explore Warren's uses of time, many of which assert some variation on the idea that Warren is constantly concerned with "the need for one to accept the past if he is to live meaningfully in the present" (Brooks, 1986, p. 27). This view of time and memory, however, is a characteristic so often attached to Southern writers since the Civil War that it has almost become platitudinal; to make this statement about Warren's use of time is almost akin to explaining his poetry by saying that he is from Kentucky. Not only is this particular subject one that Warren never exhausted, but it deserves to be examined carefully, especially in regards to late poems like "Old-Time Childhood in Kentucky," "Old Photograph of the Future," and "Covered Bridge." In eighty-four years, Robert Penn Warren surely saw enough time and wrote enough about it to move beyond what has become a stereotypically "Southern" understanding of the past, present, and future, and his discussions of memory and identity in poetry are especially interesting regarding the formation of the self.

In order to explore the role of time in Warren's poetry, one must first consider what the term means to him. The definition offered by *Webster's Ninth New Collegiate Dictionary* that is most similar to Warren's concept of time calls it "a continuum which lacks spatial dimensions and in which events succeed one another from past through present to future" (1990, p. 1235). To Warren, time is something separate and inhuman. It is an independent entity with which man coexists, struggles, and measures the changes and events he experiences. Time is not so much a player in the game of life as it is the field on which the game is played; it only seems "savage" and "innocent" at times because it is "morally neutral" (Berner, 1980, p. 68). Because man is in the motion of history through a stationary time, Warren is able to use it in his work as a series of reference points from which to formulate a concept of the self, much in the way Grumet or Pinar might recommend. While race, class, and gender are more popular factors of identity determination today, Warren uses time to construct the nature of the self, believing an understanding of the ways in which one changes over time to be "essential to successful self definition" (Clements, 1981, p. 229). In the great "continuum" of time that man walks through, Warren begins his search for identity by stepping out of line, looking behind him and in front of him in an attempt to figure out exactly where and who he is. As A. L. Clements says, "a man in Time cannot know the end, cannot know until he is out of Time" (p. 220), so Warren in his poetry "abstracts himself" (Dickey, 1984, p. 82) from time in certain frozen moments that he hopes will help make sense of his identity as a whole.

This method of defining the self is necessarily dependent on a sensitive memory, which Warren uses "combined with the discoveries achieved in maturity to provide insight toward the relationship between the self and what John Crowe Ransom called 'the world's body'" (Corrigan, 1999, p. 157). Since in Warren's poetry, "any event in time is meaningful only in relation to past and future events" (Clements, 1981, p. 228), the idea is to pull one moment frozen in memory out of sequence in order to better see its meaning in relation to the nature of one's self. While Cleanth Brooks (1986) and others are certainly correct in emphasizing the importance of the past in Warren's work, the shortcoming of their expression of this idea is that it only seems to include history, or the events and actions in which man participates. Warren's view of time does include history, but it is also conscious of the "continuum" described in Webster's definition; history is made up of the events that happen *in* time and are captured in memory. The process of finding identity through time for Warren works much like a library, with the time continuum being the shelves, memories being the books on those shelves, and history being the information contained in those books. Once Warren "abstracts himself" from time, he then becomes a visitor to the library who takes down one volume from the shelves in an attempt to better understand the nature of the series which makes up his life. While merely stepping out of the historical line of all men helps Warren define himself against them in a negative sense (who he is not), examining his own history through the books of memory, much as Pinar might, helps the poet define himself in a positive sense (who he is). As Richard Jackson puts it, the whole picture of time "becomes known by the differences established between discontinuous moments, experienced by a central self which yet finds 'definition' in that very experience" (1980, p. 62). Three different ways of examining this process are found in "Old-Time Childhood," "Old Photograph," and "Covered Bridge."

7

"Old-Time Childhood in Kentucky" (1998) shows a narrator using the library of time effectively, whether he finds what he is looking for or not. Here, as in the other two poems, the narrator is an older man looking far back through time into his childhood, hoping to understand who he has become in the present and why. The narrator's memory in this poem works splendidly, recalling vivid details like "the pink inner flesh of black fingers/Crushing to green juice tobacco worms plucked/From a leaf" (lines 3–5). He remembers clearly the books he read to his grandfather (line 25), words that were spoken in his youth, and even details like "The marks of the old man's stick in the dust" (line 22). The use of memory here is more successful than in the other two poems; when the narrator speaks with full confidence of "the encroachment of shadow" (line 40) so long ago or his childhood visit to the cave with his uncle and grandfather, it is indeed like he is reading from a book or describing events that happened just yesterday. His memory is almost photographic at some points, capturing "The great trout,/Motionless, poised in the shadow of his/Enormous creek-boulder" (lines 6–8). The narrator's powers of recollection, at their most effective, are even better than a photograph, moving deeper than just events and pictures into the richer realm of thoughts, dreams, and feelings. He does not just remember the circumstances surrounding General Jackson's duel for honor, but can still feel what it was like to struggle with that concept, how he "longed to understand" (lines 16–17) what it meant.

What is perhaps even more interesting than the narrator's ability to remember as an older man is his ability to understand time and the world as a young man. The narrator begins the poem by saying that "When I was a boy I saw the world I was in./I saw it for what it was" (lines 1–2). Though this statement sounds at first like a young man's thoughts filtered through an old man's experience and wisdom, the rest of the poem soon pushes the audience back toward an honest reading of the first two lines. The memories that follow these lines are the poem's most visual and photographic, all discontinuous flashes of the present. The images of canebrakes, tobacco, and the "great trout" are, truly, the world as it "was"; that is, the world as it existed in those exact moments. For the narrator, the world in his childhood was one of immediacy, one that only existed in the *now*. However, this world of the present eventually changed when, as the narrator says, "the past and future broke on me, as I got older" (line 9).

The young man grows into the past first (line 10), which Brooks would agree is not at all "Strange," if he is to grow and live properly in the future. In fact, the boy does all the right things in order to understand the past: he handles "the old bullet-mold" (line 10), he studies history (stanza 3), he listens to his elders and asks them questions. The narrator-child also ponders strategies (line 19) and motivations (General Jackson), searching beyond the facts of history and into the minds of those who created it. He even tries in his youth to comprehend "the magic word" (line 17), honor, in order to understand the spell that it casts on men. However, despite his attempts to make sense out of history, when his grandfather explains to him through the fossils in the cave that this was "'All once under water'" (line 31), he is at a loss. Soon, the boy sees that the "world runs the risk of meaninglessness" (Runyon, 1990, p. 59), and he asks his grandfather, "'what do you do, things being like this?'" (line 33). This struggle with a typically adult idea and resulting conversation with the grandfather are what makes the audience trust the narrator's claim that he knew the world "for what it was" in the first line. The grandfather replies,

> Love
> Your wife, love your get, keep your word, and
> If need arises die for what men die for. There aren't
> Many choices.
> And remember that truth doesn't always live in the number of voices.
> (lines 34–38)

Though the grandfather's attempt at clarification is a noble one, it is maybe too simple for the narrator-old man, whose ambivalent tone throughout the poem suggests that he has still not resolved the issue.

After answering the narrator, the grandfather leaves him alone to think about the advice and to wonder how he can figure out what he "would be, might be" (line 47) in a possibly meaningless world. In the narrator's consideration of his grandfather's words, the audience finds him not only unusually able to access time and history through memory, but also to become part of foreign stretches of it through imagination. The narrator-child simply stands in the darkness, throws his head back and his arms out, and is fantastically transported "eons back" (line 45) in time. The boy's answer to the problem of finding identity in the midst of meaninglessness seems to involve blurring the boundaries of his own time and memory in an effort to position himself in the grand range of *all* time, even moving beyond human experience. To return to the library analogy, the boy effectively takes the series of books on his life and moves them to a place on the shelves that he feels is better suited to his pursuit of self. He is not satisfied by simply *seeing* the crinoid stems; he wants to understand what it is like to *be* them. He imagines that he belongs to the time "no saying the millions/Of years" (lines 31–32) ago, alive "in that submarine/Depth and lightlessness" (lines 45–46). From this point in time, the boy feels he might be able to eventually "discover/What (he) would be" (lines 46–47), possibly hoping that the crinoid stems existed before the world became meaningless. Jackson would say that the narrator-child feels that this is possible because, in Warren's poetic world, "we can re-begin in time; we can invent the history by which we will structure our futures" (1980, p. 163). To Warren, all times are accessible, because the "past is not separate and completed in itself but an ever-developing part of a changing present and future" (Clements, 1981, p. 228). As "Old-Time Childhood" shows, this sort of access to the whole of time seems to begin in the past and depend on memory (occasionally aided by imagination), and the narrator here is in no short supply.

8

In "Old Photograph of the Future" (1998), the main character performs an act more literally like looking at a book of his past than in the other two poems; he is staring at a photograph of himself as a child. The situation here again involves an old man looking into his past with the hope of coming to terms with a sense of self, but this man has very different abilities than the narrator in "Old-Time Childhood." As much as the first poem was about extraordinary powers of memory, "Old Photograph" is about the lack of those powers. One way that Warren calls attention to the main character's lack of memory is by the fact that the picture of the past in this poem is not a recalled mental image (as it is in "Old-Time Childhood"), but an actual photograph. In this photograph, just as in the old man's mind, colors that were "no doubt, pink and white" (line 2) are now faded into "only a trace/Of grays" (lines 3–4). Not only is the old man reliant on the photograph for pictures of his past, but he does not even seem to be familiar with the photo itself. He can only guess at the color of his "infantile face" (line 1), and if he remembers seeing the expression on it before now, he does not recall the information (line 4).

The next two stanzas examine the images of his mother and father. However, these images are not accompanied by memories of them or stories about the picture itself. The mother is described as a "pretty and young" (line 6) woman who gazes at her infant child with a "look of surprised blessedness" (line 7), but these do not sound like the personal reflections of a son. They are, rather, little more than any stranger would say about a picture of a mother and child. Similarly, the father is said to loom behind, "face agleam with achievement and pride" (line 10). He is a "masculine figure" (line 9) who assures his family that "the world's in good hands—lay your worries aside" (line 12). Again, there are no references to lessons taught by his father or time spent with him, just as there is no mention of the mother's nurturing in the previous stanza. This family is clearly not the family from "Old-Time Childhood"; both the mother and father here are stock characters with only the classic traits of typical young parents attributed to them.

The photograph in some ways does provide the access to all times found in "Old-Time Childhood," since it belongs to the past, contains a frozen moment of the present, and depicts the infant child who is to be the "future." However, the problem for the old man in this poem is that he cannot make a connection with the photograph because it is a false memory. Even though the photo is like a book of the past for the main character, it is of no help in his search to understand himself, because he cannot claim any kind of authorship of it. To use Grumet's terms, the narrator seems stuck in the realm of biography, rather than autobiography. Any such photograph has the potential to be useful, but it would have to be accompanied by the memories and feelings necessary to make the picture a real part of his past and his identity. Since it is not enhanced by these things, it is no more a clue to the old man's understanding of self than if it were a picture of someone else's family.

The main character's separation from the image of his past brings up another important point about the lack of memory in the poem: the consequential dependence on others. The photograph is, after all, a visual memory "abstracted" from time by someone else for the main character. Dependence on others is an issue that appears early in "Old Photograph of the Future," and it is a problem for the old man that shows up in more than just memory. He is called twice in the first two stanzas "That center of attention" (lines 1 and 5), and he indeed seems to miss his parents less for being two people he loved than for the attention they gave him. To his mother he was "precious" (line 6) and a "mysterious miracle" (line 8); to his father he was something to be proud of (line 10) and to protect (line 12). The tone of the poem suggests that without them, "That center of attention" is left with only bitterness for having believed them and "guilt" (line 19) for letting them believe in him as the "future." The old man's dependence on others is also noticeable in the existence of a narrator other than the main character in the poem. As the poem unfolds, we notice that not only does the old man not tell the reader anything personal about his mother or father, but he actually does not tell him anything about himself, either. In the final stanza, the narrator reveals that the child-turned-man stands "there," not *here*, and the audience sees that the description of the photograph was, in fact, given by a stranger. This revelation shows that the thoughts in the first eighteen lines belong to the narrator, not the old man holding the photograph, and that even the main character's feelings in the final two lines are only outside interpretation. Even if the narrator is omniscient, which seems to be the case, the fact that information about the main character is second-hand is still important and suggests dependence. By the end of "Old Photograph of the Future," Warren has shown that the main character's inability to recollect worsens a position of general dependency in which he needs photographs for memories, parents to give him self-worth and protection, and a narrator to tell his story.

The old man's failure to use a frozen moment to learn anything about his identity can be explained by the fact that in Warren's work, "Self-knowledge is difficult because the self is not so much just a knowable object but rather a series of relations in time" (Clements, 1981, p. 230). The old man fails, then, because while he has the beginning of the series in the photograph and the end of it in the present, he lacks the necessary middle to draw them together. He lacks "synthesis," as Pinar (1975/1994) might put it. Without memory, he is unable to connect his past self with his present self in order to understand the whole of his identity. After seventy-five years, he is in such poor condition that "old landscapes blur" (line 19) and even the "promises unkept" that he remembers are "nameless" (line 20). He is left so detached from the past and so far from an understanding of self that even his despair is "undefinable" (line 20).

9

While the man in "Old Photograph of the Future" lacks the ability to use time and memory to understand the self, the man in "Covered Bridge" (1998) is not only able to use the process, but he also understands it well enough to analyze it. Through memory, the narrator here takes the audience back to his childhood, during which he was "another self" (line 1). While the man in "Old Photograph" also understands the concept of being two selves, the difference here is that the selves are linked. In a stanza that provides direct evidence for the "library" way of understanding

Warren's discussion of time and memory, the narrator in "Covered Bridge" claims that his two selves are connected by everything "that has happened since" (line 2), which he keeps "arranged on the shelf/Of memory in a sequence that I call Myself" (lines 3–4). These lines also speak to the fact that to Warren, understanding identity "is a process of continuous becoming" (Clements, 1981, p. 230), because the self is constantly changing as it passes through time. This is reminiscent of what Derrida says about "iterability" in an interview with John Caputo (1997), that what we have done or been one day must be done or lived again and again in order to be true; we "will have to reinaugurate, to reinvent," and "the inauguration has to be reinvented everyday" (p. 28). In Warren's concept, the narrator's complete collection of these memories creates a series of multiple selves, with each successive memory containing a different self. The resulting identity, then, is achieved by forming many different selves into one self, which is what the narrator calls "Myself." However, despite testimony in the first stanza that the narrator understands the process of defining oneself through time, his tone throughout the poem is that of an old man still unsure about his identity.

This doubt is evident in the first line of the second stanza, when the narrator begins by wondering, "How can you think back and know" who you were before the present? Here, the narrator also noticeably changes the subject of the poem from "I" to "you," signaling that his questions and experiences concerning time and identity in the following stanzas are one man's explorations meant to address a universal struggle. To start, he tries to answer his own question in the third stanza by removing a volume from his series in the library of time. In this particular chapter of his life, he remembers how he used to wonder as a child about "starlight on the river" (line 9) and whether or not the star in the sky noticed its reflection in the water. When the narrator considers the river and the star's "motionless, holy self" (line 10), he also attempts to connect process (the river) and stasis (the star), the momentary and the eternal, history and the continuum of time. The narrator feels, just as he remembers that he did in his youth, that if he could find a connection between these two things, he could somehow figure out his identity. This connection he seeks is the same one addressed in the first stanza: a link between the process of forming many selves and the one "Myself" that encompasses all of them. Apparently, being able to "call" them "Myself" (line 4) is not the same as understanding the nature of "Myself." The narrator believes one can find this connection because, in Warren's poetry, the "'presence' of past, present, and future within the horizon of the moment provides a referential structure through which the self can define its own history" (Jackson, 1988, p. 38). This effort to place all times in the "horizon of the moment" perhaps explains the narrator's fascination with the old covered bridge. The bridge in this poem works like the connection the narrator seeks, being motionless and yet representing motion. This is why the echo "of hoof or wheel" (line 15) on the bridge is able to fill "the vastness of [his] mind" (line 20), because that first "impact" (line 15) represents to the narrator the experience of being part of both history and time at once. In his own mind, the boy had not yet participated in this connection by crossing the bridge, and therefore could not yet know his identity. The narrator realizes now that this is why he used to lie awake at night, wondering when he would "proceed/To trot through the caverning dark beneath that roof" (lines 22–3). For these purposes, his destination would not have to be known, indeed could not be known; what he needed was "Just going. That would be enough" (line 24).

However, since by the time the story is being told the narrator and "you" *have* already crossed the bridge, the poem provokes a few questions. Having connected the momentary with the eternal on the bridge, why does one need to "prove identity" (line 30) by raising one's "scarcely visible" hand in the "gloom" (line 31)? If one can understand the nature of time and memory as they relate to the self (stanza 1), can extract moments from history for examination (stanzas 2–6), and can draw connections between those moments and the whole continuum of time (bridge), then why is it that one still cannot understand the nature of one's self in old age? Why doesn't Warren's narrator achieve the "synthesis" Pinar (1975/1994) describes? The answer to these questions is the same, and part of it is revealed in the last two stanzas. Even though the narrator claims to have all "that has happened since" his childhood "arranged on the shelf/Of memory" (lines 2–4), this is not entirely true. His memory has begun to slip; he states that "you" cannot now recall "What pike, highway or path" (line 28) has led "you" from place to place and time to time to where "you" are now. These lines show that even the narrator, who has been so concerned with retaining and arranging his memories, cannot remember everything. Though Lesa Corrigan speaks of "memory's timelessness" (1999, p. 145) in Warren's poetry, memory is not completely timeless. Though it is timeless in the sense that it can freeze a moment out of time, memory is only timeless, or lasting, as long as it can be recalled from storage. As Warren shows in "Covered Bridge," the trouble is that man cannot ever truly complete his library of memory, and the poet uses these verses to ask how this realization affects notions of identity and meaning. While the man in "Old-Time Childhood" is ambiguous in his answer and the man from "Old Photograph" cannot remember enough to fully address the question, the narrator of "Covered Bridge" understands and makes no pretensions about the limitations of defining oneself through memory. The real problem, the reason that the narrator looks for his hand in a panic of futility, is that he now knows that he has spent his entire life trying to define himself through what is perhaps the most unreliable of methods. The narrator writes to "you" because the fragility of what he calls "Myself" has become apparent. Since time lacks "spatial dimensions" and man is constantly moving through it, it is truly accessible only through memory; when memory fails, the series is broken, and complete identity becomes impossible. The imagination, or "creative memory" (Justus, 1981, p. 78), used with such power in "Old-Time Childhood" is really of no help in Warren's system of self-knowledge, since imaginary moments are only capable of producing imaginary identity. Realizing this, the narrator of "Covered Bridge" abandons his search for self-definition through time for the only option that he believes is available: to strain his eyes after his own hand in the darkness.

Why, then, write a book of poetry to explore memory and identity, as I have done here, if memory is an ultimately unreliable way of understanding the self? Maybe the problem is not the use of poetry to explore memory and identity, but rather the assumptions about how memory works, and how complete it can be. This "library" concept in Warren's work is fascinating as a way of thinking about time and identity, but it is also faulty, as his narrators often discover. For one, it does not fully take into account what Derrida calls "inauguration" (Caputo, 1997); in other words, yesterdays—all of them, maybe—are important, but maybe not more important than tomorrows. As he puts it, "if tomorrow you do not reinvent today's inauguration, you will be dead" (1997, p. 28). And there is always tomorrow, and tomorrow we will be someone new, at least a little different than today's version. This is something akin to what I tell my students about their insecurities over not having "read everything": even if we could read everything ever written, they'd print more books tomorrow. That certainly does not mean we should quit reading books, though, or that they can't help us figure out ourselves and the world we live in, at least a little better than we knew them before. Another important difficulty of Warren's "library" concept of identity is the incomplete nature of yesterday's records. I played four years of basketball in high school, and took it very seriously, but can't remember a single final score to a single game. On the other hand, I can tell you that a mile is made up of 5, 280 feet—or 1, 760 yards. We remember so little, really, and who knows if it's the important stuff? If I gave my students the world's best lecture on this material, and then told a good joke at the end, which would they be more likely to recall?

And this is why I think an attitude of adventure is better than one of accounting when it comes to writing poetry in order to figure out who we are; an admission of mystery instead of a quest for the "truth"; a "space of exploration, of bringing the inside out" (Morgan, 2016, p. 52). Even the "creative memory" Justus (1981) refers to can be useful, and should not be dismissed as if this were a court of law; what I imagine and the ways in which I imagine it are also valuable texts for identity formation. I do know that I have been assigning my literature and writing students to write poetry for years now, sometimes personal and sometimes less so, and it seems to be doing them a noticeable amount of good. In purely practical terms, even the ones who never come to love poetry admit that they get better at analyzing it, having had to write it themselves, much in the way an auto mechanic probably understands cars better if she has to build one herself. I also notice an improvement in their writing across the board; the strict and demanding attention to word choice and imagery, the pressure to be creative and possibly original, are good for their writing voices overall. But maybe more importantly, they gain a confidence in self-expression and an expanded self-awareness that can only help them, no matter what they do with their lives after my class. Each fall for sixteen years now, I have hosted a public poetry reading for my students, at which they perform their own work, complete with microphone, requisite overwrought coffee drinks, and plenty of nerves. Almost everyone who participates—and most of my students choose to—has never done this kind of thing before, and part of my pitch to them is "If you can read your own poetry, in public, into a microphone, and care about it, what are you going to be too scared to do after that?" They almost always find it less terrifying than they expected, and they often discover that they are better than they thought, too. I have found over the years that, like Meredith Walker says, "there is something positive about people of all kinds finding something of themselves and their world in poetry" (2016, p. 67), no matter their previous experience or future vocation.

11

Part of the reason Bruce Wexler can say that "poetry is dead" is that it just has so much competition for our attention these days, and much of that competition is loud, literally and figuratively. But I argue that while this may make poetry *unfamiliar* for many of us, it does not make it dead. In fact, poets like Billy Collins believe that this unfamiliarity can be rectified, and that much of the answer lies in making poetry a more normal, more approachable, more regular part of our lives, and this idea is one of the big reasons I assign students to write it. In *Poetry 180: A Turning Back to Poetry* (2003), Collins has assembled 180 poems—one for each day of school— that he hopes will be read as part of the morning announcements, not as part of an assignment or accompanied by teacher comments or explanation; rather, he hopes students will "just listen to a poem every morning and off you go to your first class" (p. xvi). His idea is that poetry too often seems obscure and unapproachable, and he is hopeful that this approach, with "short, clear, contemporary poems" (p. xvi), will help bring in new readers and writers who assume they don't like poetry in part because they have limited experience with it. The Poetry Society of America is one of many organizations devoted to similar ideas, in this case setting a goal of "bringing poems back into everyday life" by placing poetry placards "in the transit systems of a dozen cities across the country, reaching over thirteen million people a day" (Paschen, 2002, p. xxiii). William Louis-Dreyfus calls these poems "resting places along the road, each with its own portion of intimacy, calm, wisdom, and nourishment" (2002, p. xxii). What advocates like these seem to agree upon is that we need to live *with* poetry and live *in* poetry—we need participation.

And participation means that we cannot just read poetry more; we need to write it. This is just as true, and maybe more so, for teachers of literature and writing as it is for students. Dennis J. Sumara points out that while "in recent years there has been increased attention to the teaching of writing, in many cases writing is not being taught by writers," and further argues that this is one of the reasons that "most young people would say that neither reading nor writing literature matters" (2002, p. 157). He has a point: vocal coaches should be singers, art teachers should be artists, etc. Teachers should be intimately familiar with both the difficulties and benefits of writing, especially the creative and personal, if they want to convey those things to their students. No wonder we have a tough time selling the importance of writing when we don't do it much ourselves. So where do we find these writers to teach writing? As is often the case when we need something we are afraid we won't find, we should look in the mirror. If we do not think of ourselves as writers, we should— and then we should *become* writers. Maybe that will make us uncomfortable at first, but so what? Our students already know this discomfort all too well. Teachers are students, too, let us not forget, and often profess to be interested in passing on an attitude of lifelong learning to their students. Are we still learning, though, growing as our students do? Let us not coast, and rust, and fall into the hollow safety of clichés on kitten posters that we pretend our students don't see through. And even if poetry does not naturally come to us, we can work at writing just as our students do, to the benefit of all. To paraphrase Derrida, we might have spent years of college studying literature, but if we do not "reinaugurate" that knowledge, that skill, that participation, we will lose it, and likely our ability to make literature—or maybe much of anything else—come to life for our students. After all, as Alan A. Block says, "To live is to read texts, but to be alive is to write them" (1988/1999). And if we do finally confess our insecurity about such things, and worry that we can't do what we know we should; if it doesn't always go well, and millions of people don't clamor for our autographs, I'm just not sure it all matters very much. What matters is the doing, the making, the creating, the "singing" of the self as Whitman once urged us to, a unique voice in the chorus of mankind. As Henry Miller put it, in the preface to his water-color album called *The Angel is my Watermark* (1961/1962, p. 38), "we don't have to turn out a masterpiece every day. To paint is the thing, not to make masterpieces." So let us all write our books of poetry, masterpieces or no. Walt Whitman himself said we could "contribute a verse" (1892/1993); do we really need someone else's permission (or commission)?

12

The book of poetry that follows, called *Fireflies*, is my way of putting my poetry where my theory is. This work is an example of the kind of "*liminal*" scholarship I advocate in *The Need for* Revision (2011), occupying a space in the academic world's "windows and doorways" (p. 2), not exactly in any one field but rather in the "spaces-between where the inside and outside commingle"; it seeks to trouble the boundaries between teacher and writer, critic and artist, writer and reader, and teacher and student in a way from which I hope all parties might benefit. The intended audience for this book is anyone who works with or is interested in poetry, curriculum theory, secondary public education, literature, the humanities in general, or any combination thereof. Specifically, this group would include curriculum scholars, teachers and students of literature and other humanities courses, and curriculum directors. And while this work is not a textbook, exactly, it is also intended for use as a course text in teacher preparation programs like Curriculum Studies, Curriculum and Instruction, and English Education, both at the undergraduate and graduate levels. This is a book of poetry, but it is also a book about poetry, and about how much we need poetry to play a larger role in all our lives—about how we need to live more poetically. As such, it is intended to be an approachable text about big ideas and issues that can be useful and appropriate in a variety of settings.

Fireflies is a book about memory, and the way each year is full of many years; it is about the way memory makes us who we are, despite the fact that it isn't comprehensive, or chronological, or even stable, but rather comes to us in little flashes, like fireflies in the dusk. It is a work inspired by the poetry of Robert Penn Warren, Billy Collins, Jean Toomer, and Fred Chappell as well as Carl Leggo and Sandra L. Faulkner, and keeps as a guiding principle Whitman's notion of the "Song of Myself" that is really the song of everyone, beginning with the personal but aiming for the communal, the shared experience. The book is made up of three sections, each one corresponding to a four-month period of the year. Each poem in each section is nestled in that part of the year, whether by events or imagery or thematic association. In this way the book plays loosely with time, just as memory does; "A Light Blanket" is set in the fall season generally, "New Hope" was inspired by a specific date from a specific spring that lingers and affects me many years after, and "Wine-Dark Seas" is about every May of my life—and maybe lots of people's lives. And while the idea for the book began with "Dance of the Ancients," inspired by my thirtieth birthday and an impulse to do some personal stock-taking, it has become something that moves both backward and forward in time from there; sometimes the memories are about being a young boy, and sometimes about being the father of a young boy. Some of the poems are pretty directly about school, as both student and teacher, and some are more about the kind of things I bring with me into the classroom whether they are in my lesson plans or not. The poems, like memories, are both distinct, individual flashes—fireflies—without clear context, and also the pieces we use to build what we call ourselves.

I hope you like it, I hope it resonates with you and your own experience—but mostly I hope you go looking for your pens.

REFERENCES

Abrams, M. H. (1999). *A glossary of literary terms* (7th ed.). Fort Worth, TX: Harcourt Brace College Publishers.
Berner, R. (1980). The required past: World enough and time. In R. Gray (Ed.), *Robert Penn Warren: A collection of critical essays* (pp. 67–75). Englewood Cliffs, NJ: Prentice-Hall, Inc.
Block, A. A. (1999). The answer is blowin' in the wind: A deconstructive reading of the school text. In W. F. Pinar (Ed.), *Contemporary curriculum discourses: Twenty years of JCT* (pp. 177–198). New York, NY: Peter Lang. (Original work published 1988)
Bloom, H. (1998). Foreword. In J. Burt (Ed.), *The collected poems of Robert Penn Warren*. Baton Rouge, LA: Louisiana University Press.
Brooks, C. (1986). R. P. Warren: Experience redeemed in knowledge. In H. Bloom (Ed.), *Modern critical views: Robert Penn Warren* (pp. 27–47). New York, NY: Chelsea House.
Caputo, J. (1997). *Deconstruction in a nutshell: A conversation with Jacques Derrida.* New York, NY: Fordham University Press.
Clements, A. L. (1981). Sacramental vision: The poetry of Robert Penn Warren. In W. B. Clark (Ed.), *Critical essays on Robert Penn Warren* (pp. 216–233). Boston, MA: G. K. Hall and Company.

Corrigan, L. C. (1999). Poetry, 1970–1985. In *Poems of pure imagination: Robert Penn Warren and the romantic tradition* (pp. 141–160). Baton Rouge, LA: Louisiana State University Press.

Dickey, J. (1984). Warren's poetry: A reading and commentary. In W. B. Edgar (Ed.), *A southern renaissance man: Views of Robert Penn Warren*. Baton Rouge, LA: Louisiana State University Press.

Dylan Thomas. (2011). In J. Allen et al. (Eds.), *McDougal Littell literature: British literature* (p. 1158). Evanston, IL: McDougal Littell.

Faulkner, S. L. (2014). *Family stories, poetry, and women's work: Knit four, frog one (poems)*. Rotterdam: Sense Publishers.

Grumet, M. R. (1999). Autobiography and reconceptualization. In W. F. Pinar (Ed.), *Contemporary curriculum discourses: Twenty years of JCT* (pp. 24–30). New York, NY: Peter Lang. (Original work published 1980)

Heaney, S. (1998). Digging. In *Opened ground: Poems 1966–1996*. New York, NY: Farrar, Straus and Giroux. (Original work published 1966)

Hegel, G. W. (1993). *Introductory lectures on aesthetics* (B. Bosanquet, Trans. & M. Inwood, Ed.). London: Penguin Books. (Original work published 1886)

Hofstadter, A. (1971). Introduction. In M. Heidegger (Ed.), *Poetry, language, thought* (A. Hofstadter, Trans.). New York, NY: HarperCollins.

Housman, A. E. (1993). Terence, this is stupid stuff. In M. H. Abrams (Ed.), *The Norton anthology of English literature* (Vol. 2., 6th ed.). New York, NY: W. W. Norton & Company. (Original work published 1896)

Hughes, L. (2002). Cross. In T. R. Arp & G. Johnson (Eds.), *Perrine's literature: Structure, sound, and sense* (8th ed.). Boston, MA: Heinle & Heinle. (Original work published 1926)

Jackson, R. (1980). The shards of time: Robert Penn Warren and the moment of the self: A review essay. *Southern Humanities Review, 14*(2), 161–167.

Jackson, R. (1988). The generous time: Robert Penn Warren and the phenomenology of the moment. In *The dismantling of time in contemporary poetry* (pp. 1–64). Tuscaloosa, AL: University of Alabama Press.

John Keats. (2011). In J. Allen et al. (Eds.), *McDougal Littell literature: British literature* (p. 860). Evanston, IL: McDougal Littell.

Justus, J. H. (1981). Visions and speculations: 1957–1980. In *The achievement of Robert Penn Warren* (pp. 69–113). Baton Rouge, LA: Louisiana State University Press.

Kirsh, A. (2016, April). The patron saint of inner lives. *The Atlantic*, pp. 38–40.

Leggo, C. (2012). *Sailing in a concrete boat: A teacher's journey*. Rotterdam: Sense Publishers.

Lord Byron. (2011). In J. Allen et al. (Eds.), *McDougal Littell literature: British literature* (p. 832). Evanston, IL: McDougal Littell.

Louis-Dreyfus, W. (2002). Preface. In E. Paschen & B. F. Lauer (Eds.), *Poetry in motion from coast to coast*. New York, NY: W. W. Norton & Company.

Matthew Arnold. (2011). In J. Allen et al. (Eds.), *McDougal Littell literature: British literature* (p. 1034). Evanston, IL: McDougal Littell.

Miller, H. (1962). The angel is my watermark. In *Stand still like the hummingbird* (pp. 38–41). New York: New Directions. (Original work published 1961)

Morgan, O. (2016, April). [Commentary on national poetry month] (pp. 52–53). Poetry.

Olds, S. (1999). Take the I out. In *Blood, Tin, Straw*. New York, NY: Alfred A. Knopf.

Owen, Jr., D. P. (2011). *The need for revision: Curriculum, literature, and the 21st century*. Rotterdam: Sense Publishers.

Paschen, E. (2002). Introduction. In E. Paschen & B. F. Lauer (Eds.), *Poetry in motion from coast to coast*. New York, NY: W. W. Norton & Company.

Percy Shelley. (2011). In J. Allen et al. (Eds.), *McDougal Littell literature: British literature* (p. 846). Evanston, IL: McDougal Littell.

Pinar, W. F. (1994). The method of currere. In *Autobiography, politics and sexuality: Essays in curriculum theory 1972–1992* (pp. 19–28). New York, NY: Peter Lang. (Original work published 1975)

Robert Browning. (2011). In J. Allen et al. (Eds.), *McDougal Littell literature: British literature* (p. 924). Evanston, IL: McDougal Littell.

Robertson, R. (Producer), & Scorsese, M. (Director). (1978). *The last waltz* [Motion picture]. United States: MGM.

Runyon, R. P. (1990). *The braided dream: Robert Penn Warren's late poetry.* Lexington, KY: University Press of Kentucky.

Samuel Taylor Coleridge. (2011). In J. Allen et al. (Eds.), *McDougal Littell literature: British literature* (pp. 796–825). Evanston, IL: McDougal Littell.

Shelley, P. B. (1977). A defence of poetry. In D. H. Reiman & S. B. Powers (Eds.), *Shelley's poetry and prose.* New York, NY: W. W. Norton & Company. (Original work published 1840)

Sumara, D. J. (2002). *Why reading literature in school still matters: Imagination, interpretation, insight.* Mahwah, NJ: Lawrence Erlbaum Associates.

Time. (1990). In F. C. Mish (Ed.), *Webster's ninth new collegiate dictionary* (p. 1235). Springfield, MA: Merriam-Webster Inc.

T. S. Eliot. (2011). In J. Allen et al. (Eds.), *McDougal Littell literature: British literature* (p. 1092). Evanston, IL: McDougal Littell.

Walker, M. (2016, April). *Smart girls read poetry* (pp. 65–67). Poetry.

Warren, R. P. (1998). Covered bridge. In J. Burt (Ed.), *The collected poems of Robert Penn Warren.* Baton Rouge, LA: Louisiana University Press.

Warren, R. P. (1998). Old photograph of the future. In J. Burt (Ed.), *The collected poems of Robert Penn Warren.* Baton Rouge, LA: Louisiana University Press.

Warren, R. P. (1998). Old-time childhood in Kentucky. In J. Burt (Ed.), *The collected poems of Robert Penn Warren.* Baton Rouge, LA: Louisiana University Press.

Wexler, B. (2003, May 5). Poetry is dead. Does anybody really care? *Newsweek*, p. 18.

Whitman, W. (1993). O me! O life! In *Leaves of grass.* New York, NY: Random House. (Original work published 1892)

Whitman, W. (1993). Song of myself. In *Leaves of grass.* New York, NY: Random House. (Original work published 1892)

Whitman, W. (1993). Song of the open road. In *Leaves of grass.* New York, NY: Random House. (Original work published 1892)

William Blake. (2011). In J. Allen et al. (Eds.), *McDougal Littell literature: British literature* (p. 752). Evanston, IL: McDougal Littell.

William Wordsworth. (2011). In J. Allen et al. (Eds.), *McDougal Littell literature: British literature* (p. 782). Evanston, IL: McDougal Littell.

Williams, R. (1970). The romantic artist. In R. Gleckner & G. Enscoe (Eds.), *Romanticism: Points of view* (pp. 269–285). Englewood Cliffs, NJ: Prentice Hall. (Original work published 1962)

FIREFLIES

A PREAMBLE

Some days I write to breathe,

the last few curves and stems
of letters barely legible
in the gasp
of trying to eat the sky,
to swallow, to digest, to absorb,
to achieve the fullness that leads
to solvency, to dissipation.
To disappear. To become.

I know it is a lot to ask
of paper, of pen.
Besides, am I really that
fragile?

Yes.

We all are, all the same—
except I will say it
while you, you will be "fine,"
and they, they
all turn away and laugh and lie
with all but their eyes
but I,
I will look.
I will see. I will know.
And some days I will lose,
but not every day.

Shortness of breath
is just a preamble.

JANUARY—FEBRUARY—MARCH—APRIL

DANCE OF THE ANCIENTS

What to say of three decades?
I hope I get three more.
But for now, I think I'll just lie
on the couch near the windows
and watch the tall trees rock
to a slow waltz, brushed by
currents in the air that I
can't reach yet, while I try
very hard to do nothing,
be nothing—just for a few
minutes—timing my breathing
by the dance of the ancients.

EACH MORNING IS A GIFT

Each morning is a gift,
whether it is wrapped
in thin blues and greens,
covered in blankets of
whispering gray, or
bathed in showers of
blessed translucence.
But the ones I like best
begin with deep color,
with new hues so
full-blooded and rich
I am surprised at their
boldness, the confidence
of their voices, as if
the sky that is already
so vast, mysterious, limitless,
is reminding me that it
can be even more,
if it wants to,
and at any moment.

FOUR MINUTES

No one gets that
to drive to work at 6:45
is pure bliss,

four minutes of the near-silence
that lets me hear for another
day, the hum of the motor

taking its place alongside
the earth's own chirps, buzzes—
heartbeats of the world waking.

And some days, almost
never the ones I expect,
God's smile is full-toothed,

so wide in the sky over the
river I can't see it all,
though I know what it means

and wink in response,
sleepily.

STILL

If I could just stop
halfway across the parking lot
when my aging Ford is pointed
directly at the face of God
as it rises over the treeline,
eyes wide and full of listening
and telling both and knowing
what that kind of stillness
might mean to me. If I
could just stop.

But those eyes also know
in blue that almost isn't
that I can't, yet;
I have things to do still,
and so that gaze
never holds me for long,
clears off so that my breath
returns, lets me loose from
under the impossible weight.

THE WAY LIGHT LOOKS

I don't think light should
look like that, but
I like it, the way it
breaks and splinters
over clouds, spilling color
instead of caressing warmly
the cool morning blue,
tempering the tantrums
of Georgia afternoon.

But then I guess light
doesn't *look*, in either
way you're thinking
(English teachers!)
but rather makes us
look, selflessness elemental,
the show of the show.

God, the beauty of it all
(No Mom, I'm not swearing).

SHADOWS ON THE SIDEWALK

The day is as indifferent to me as it ever was.

Cool mornings are explained away,
and the sun is
not *love*,
not *hate*,
just *heat*,
and never guaranteed.

What's more, I can be indifferent, too,
and match his detachment with cool distance,
unflappable. I will see his February chill,
and raise him.

I will wake with a title fight in my head.
I will treat him like an obstacle to be overcome,
like shadows on the sidewalk,
or age.
I will black his eye. I will bloody his nose.
And when his jab is finally exposed for the sophistry
it has always been,
I will break his will.
Or my hand.
And then swing again.

The day is as indifferent to me as it ever was.

MORNING IN NEW ORLEANS

Lone jazzman,
Mississippi riverboat behind:
a postcard to nowhere
from no one.
Sun that shines gold
on brass and brown skin
alike, the saxophone
like a smile extended,
a kiss of the air made
suddenly solid.
At no one's request
and selling only life,
bloodflow, chestswell,
he blows notes into
sky so clear they
take form too,
burn to life,
become, tangible, colored
things with shape and
hue that hold and turn
before me, until
caught by February
breeze and blown again,
scattered ashes and sparks
of holy fire unto
the world.

TWO INCHES OF SNOW

The second of two days
off school, only patches
of light left and less snow.
Two-year-old you is standing
bundled on the deck of
your playhouse, peeking over
the railing and knocking
off icicles with mittened hands,
each one a sharp pillar
of frozen time ticking
and a frosted window cylinder
showing my face lined with
age but yours, yours I
can't quite see reflected, always just
turned away and turning.
At the top of the slide
you say "Daddy, catch me"
but I'd swear you
were asking me to help
you load your car.

FORSYTHIA

An explosion of ur-yellow
caught and held at the flashpoint,
nature glorious unruly asymmetric,
as untamed and untranslatable
as Whitman, growing
like jazz into the night.
And if I listen carefully
enough I swear I will
hear it sing in a rhythm
untaught a melody as yet unheard,
its own barbaric yawp,
sudden and free,
and one day I'll sing with it a
harmony only God could love.

But make no mistake—
He *will* love it.

GREEN

There is a tint of green
that only exists after
warm-weather rain,

and I want to live there,
with soft sun and clear
breeze, listening to trees

whisper the day's secrets,
older than I'll ever be,
and younger than I can wish.

GROWTH

In the dark and quiet
when I listen to her
breathing I feel my
self sink, down through
the floor and into the
soil, fingers and toes
spreading like roots
until they grow up
into the cool night
and sway in the breeze
her lungs blow, and then
bloom again each day
in the morning light of
her eyes' open blue.

THE SMALL ONE

Yesterday
you grabbed my
finger in your
tiny little hand
and dragged me
to the laundry room
window to see the
"big truck"
—well, that's what
you meant, anyway—
that was hauling
away the last few
broken pieces of
what used to be our
driveway to make way
for the next phase of
our always new old home
but
all I could see
was your tiny shape
reflected in the window
pane, the glow of
sun and son
glazing glass on
which your little
pointing finger left
smudges that made
me feel like the
small one

THE DISTANCE

Sometimes I want words to end words,
to say it once and need it said no more,
silence the prize of perfection—
and then I remember myself,
that the flaw is the fun,
the distance the design,
that word will never hold world,
and thank God for that.

PHAETHON

The hum of daylight
when you're not ready for it.
I rise, stumble, head full
and empty and heavy,
and the window shows me
that Saturday's electric sun
is really my father
working.

I am stronger than he is
(in the way that I know strength),
teenage athlete, capable.
Unasked.
And I know, but
cannot figure out how to express
it, or return it, despite that
medal the school gave me—
I know that I am loved.

I roll over and sleep until adulthood,
hoping to awake a man,
hoping that man will have the
answers this boy does not,
hoping I can learn to take
Hyperion's reigns
and light the world for him.

HUMIDITY

Awake in a cloud, or smoke,
or potato soup, for all I know.
Locked in a downy cell,
or adrift, my own little pine-tree icemass
of suburbia exiled in the night
from the comfort of the
Nice Neighborhood Nation.

There is something disconcerting about fog,
but especially on Sundays,
like rain on Easter,
or a late December heatwave.
Frustration, confusion, fear
of things
not lining up *as they should.*
I am normally thankful
for any change in the air, no matter
when it visits me on the calendar
(who's to say when Sunday comes,
after all?),
but it's easier to sing the song of the spheres
if you can hear it with your own ears
once in a while.

But then,
I must admit the limits
of my capacity for clarity.
Too much cloudless sky
burns the earth, dries our souls,
peels my layers in the heat,
cracks me open in the cold,
exposes me
too much, too fast,
sends me seeking the dark, the wet,
the shade, the saturation.

Maybe I need the moisture—
maybe we all do.
Maybe in the fog, when I can't see,
I see myself—
maybe.

ATMOSPHERICAL

the wonder is
that the weatherman is ever right
edges of the world cracked
and crumbling patterns barely
there in movements ever
mutable in symphonies written
and unwritten striking keys
never still and still beautiful
beauty full and kinetic
power of potential
threat and promise of the possible
the wonder is

TO LOOK UP

The slow walk up the driveway.
Night darkness and
tree root cracks hidden
until *here* and then
the next *here* and the
ones that reach up jagged
crumbling to catch my
toe *here* and what I
want is to look up
instead of down to see
what runes of constellation
tonight are framed by
old pine tree sentinel sway
and the south roof line,
what messages are written for
me in wispy cloud wandering
and whispering stray wind,
what notes are dropped here and
there drifting on breezes
I too often fail to catch.

ILLUMINATED

Some early mornings in March,
just after the time changes,
God lets William Blake
have the sky for a half hour
or so, and the rest of us
stand in silhouetted silence
etched with flaming vision,
and the sign above the door
at the end of the hall says "exit"
but I already have.

RESURRECTION

I have heard of people
frightened of furniture,
and I believe it,
because wood is
Holy.
God is in there.
First in trees tall, stoic,
then in altar, pew, instrument, cross;
but also in house, chair, table, bed.
Beauty cut down
but also reformed,
made new.
Yes, that's right:
resurrected.
Look closely at the grain,
brown and gold river of soul
running just under glassy sheen.

No day can be the same
after this.

BECOMING

Only when I read Whitman
does death seem easy,
pleasant even, not something to fight,
not the end of things but just
the next thing, we having been
always part of everything
that ever happened and just
needing to realize what we are,
and will be, each atom belonging
to me as good belonging to you,
memories just washed clean
to make room for the world's
ever becoming.

ON THE DEATH OF MY GREAT-GRANDFATHER

I walked her back
in the absurdity of support
for sixty-nine years torn asunder
by the God who made them
inseparable.

She wasn't supposed to see
(I'm protecting her now)
the backhoe
you see.

But Death would have his moment
if he could not have more
and so I could only close the
car door, burying her, too
temporarily
in her own coffin of motion
in stasis.

She stared ahead but saw no road—
only the back of a Ford.
It was clear that when
he left he took his half
from the middle.

The circle, the cycle, the world
had stopped
in mockery or honor
but soon it would move again.

NEW HOPE

I.

As a boy once I jumped
the fence awhile to
wander lands unknown,
whose I couldn't have
guessed, and this being
long before I knew the
land really owned us.

In cow silence I walked,
head high in the morning sun,
directionless until the small
pool, shaded and still, asked
me to leave my no-path.

The cool, dark earth there invited
me so I knelt and dug,
until I pulled history
from its hiding places, fossilized
for me, and held to the sun
the faces of ghosts etched
in small stone.

The high priests of my
ceremony chewed their cud
in wise stare, certification,
and I ran home a conqueror
to tell the ghosts' stories.

II.

Years later I returned
to walk those roads for
the last time, head bowed,
hot sun on my neck,
not looking, this being

long after lands could be
unknown.

In numb silence I
buried us all to
rest eternally in the
gravel-drive shade
of a rusted metal swing.

With new-calloused
hands I put history
in its hiding places,
fossilized, then shielded
my eyes from the
sun that showed me
the faces of ghosts.

And as the high priests
looked away I wondered
about another boy digging,
about what marks we
might have left in the rock.

O LIFE

What are you, O life?
(of the questions of these recurring)
And why?
And if there are parts to play,
what is mine?
In your dawns and dusks
I have trouble telling
if the days are short
or long.

The other morning I stepped
on a spider in the dark
and wondered what
his plans had been that day
and if he were happy
he'd spent so many years
in college or watched
so much football.

I'll tell you what, though:
I bet when he could find
a minute to sit quiet
and kiss the head of his
sleeping son before returning
to his wife downstairs—
I bet he didn't ask
so many questions.

And maybe that's an answer.

IT IS WELL WITH MY SOUL

On the best days I can see
and feel the notes rise
from the piano, each one
heartbeat-timed, sound swirling
full and floating, fractal
currents coursing color carousel
and the life I forget
for the moment seems filled
with them when the music ends
and my breath begins again.

COFFEE IN ATHENS

I don't know why I expected
to see the face of Jesus
in a flaming coffee cup,
but when you're eighteen
you'll look anywhere:
words scratched on a table,
cracks in old buildings,
afternoon sidewalk trees,
a meaningful glance on the bus
held just too long.

And definitely, definitely in
the way the air feels just
before the day really gets started,
before the world begins to hum.

I saw most of life, then,
through the film of coffee steam,
fighting ever-present exhaustion
of senses and soul, like
the world might slip away
suddenly behind the veil of
closed eyelids—even in a blink.

And of course, it did:
caramel concoctions cooled,
cups emptied, shades
of light and breezes passed
with the fickle weather
and quiet tick of time.

But the steam, the vapor,
was the thing, just to
breathe it in, and God:
he was there, too, everywhere
I looked.

CURTAINS

"You don't know me," she says,
and she's right, though I only
see it just now, and not because
of her arguments. I see the curtain,
the director, just over her shoulder,
blink painfully in the hot lights,
and know finally that these are
our *parts*, not our *lives*, vaguely
remembering my worries that an
audience seemed to laugh all along,
and in the wrong spots.

So what now? Stay in character?
Cry? They'd love that, devote
an extra inch of column to the
emotion of my performance.
There are more lines, but I won't
say them, even though she'll hate me
for it, since she still hasn't seen the script,
won't know it's better this way.
No, I'll stop now, stand, look the
orchestra in the eye, exit the stage
by the footlights, walk up the center aisle,
shake hands with the mountain who wrote
this, and leave, with no goodbye,
no bow.
Enough.

FAULKNER CALLED IT KILROY

A mark here. A scratch
there.

Not much, and not for you. And not
for me.

Maybe just some lines, a little shading,
a wisp of white in the sky over
tall grass that a young boy will
say looks like a dog. A horse.

A mark here. A scratch
there.

Not much, and not for you. And not
for me.

Maybe just a note from a living
dead man, like the tapes of
my ancestors that lie on my shelf
and burn in their silence into the
back of my brain. Them, I can
see, paused, mouths open as
if to draw breath for
the tale to come.

And then a young girl who will
be seventy any second asks, "Should
I keep the doodles in the Margin, too?"
Oh, yes. Especially those.

A mark here. A scratch
there.

For the life to come.

Some part of me still stands in the yard,
having just studied the ancient Egyptians,
and with my father's pocketknife
carves at an old door, wood laid
bare so the air seeps in.

PRE-SCHOOL

I remember mostly magnolia
squatting shade silent close
to the ground leaves blown
the pages of my book turning
gathering daffodils for you
with green hands how little
we have to give and how much

HIGHWAY 52

What is it about old red brown barns
that makes them so perfectly alive
out of car windows?

Factory-steel door like a frame.

Sometimes I think I'd like to stop,
walk the hills,
swim in the thick sky awhile,
bathe in the tall grass.
And maybe, if it was April,
the wind might blow
just like you want it to,
intermittently,
partners with the sun,
a world on climate control.

But I never do stop,
and I probably won't.
No, I know too much of irony
to turn down gravel drives anymore.

And so I'll stay behind the wheel,
little god of my no-place,
where the breeze turns on a plastic knob
and time is literally at my feet.
Later, without even noticing,
I'll roll up the window when
I see chicken houses,
turn up the radio that plays
an album with an egg on the cover.

MAY—JUNE—JULY—AUGUST

WINE-DARK SEAS

May.

And all it takes is for
Joe Robert Kirkman to
mention wine-dark seas
before they rush in on me
all at once, too heavy
on my chest to breathe
easy and when I do it's
all salt-air that blows in
rhythm and light that
won't stay still, dancing
on the back of my eyelids
and soon the people rush in
too carrying bags and umbrellas
while they absent-mindedly kick
sand off the hallway tile
onto my nice shoes that wipe
away with the sand when
I brush them to expose
tanned feet that spread
brown up my legs chest shoulders
as I look up just in time to see
the black V of birds
ducking the doorways
and just when foamy green rolls
in from around the far corner
I'm sucked instantly away
200 miles by a ringing bell.

SOMEAREKEATS

Man, Grecian Urns.
You know, I'm with you, Keats:
I never know what I'm
looking at, either.
But sometimes I think it's
me that's frozen—
no time to kiss the wife
let alone have a picnic,
and when I turn the
dial I can't ever find
that good music
I just know is out there somewhere.
Of course, maybe I wouldn't like it,
either. Think that's a Wilco song.

But like I was saying,
I just don't think I'm getting
anywhere except old, and
I don't think anybody's
going to stick me in some museum.

Not sure I'd like everybody
looking at me, for that matter.
Maybe that's all I know,
and all I need to know.

Anyway,
it's just a dream I keep having,
and it doesn't seem
to mean anything.

I WRITE

People always ask
if I write.
Of course I write.
Don't you?

I write in night darkness,
by electric lamplight
looking for glowing
embers in the ether
by their trails of
shadow smoke.

I write on boat prow,
the slap! of the rhythm
breaking and building,
destroying and restoring
the story, a symbol sea
tossed by tempest and
sun-baked.

I write in rental vans,
melting Mexican-marked
and idling ivory island ones,
staring straight out at land
that doesn't love me.
I wish it would.

I write in rain rattle
of panes, pain in my
heart of hearts for the
hollow sound of the roof,
hoping hope is enough.

I write, and show it
to no one.

OF COURSE

I was in Avon, North Carolina,
the Outer Banks,
when the world ended.
And Frost and countless others
were all wrong:
no fire, no ice, no explosion,
no last grip of the sword hilt
in the face of eternity.
Rather, I just got out of
the shower and it was only us,
from the dunes to the row of
houses behind, and the rest
was a great milk-white nothing,
though a nothing made of
ghost-smoke-mist that stealthily
slipped ever inward to fill the
cracks in the deck, under the door,
into the corners of all rooms
until it was just me, still,
because I didn't know whether
to walk or swim, or call out
for—what? But I did call
out, and He answered, of course.

SAN GERVASIO

Only stones left.

Men and gods,
cares and cures, cash and culture
consumed
by time and terror
and waiting for the end of an endless world.

The altar vacant.
No priest (or manic street preacher)
to instill some fears and stay others
in people not around to have them.

Do the things we feel exist without us?

There, on the temple mound where
Maya, Mexico, America—
Man—
has died,
there exists life.

There, where the stone sits and
does not speak or feel,
there is love.

In the cracks of all that is left
and all that will be,
sways one flower,
growing
in the cold way that only a flower can,
growing.

ST. JOHN

Sea so blue it would be
a pleasure to drown,
if I could swallow it all
and live to be part of it,
boundless and blue.

Off the boat and into a jeep.
A jeep? What did I expect?
Walking? Dirt roads? Horses?
I can't ride a horse. But I
can't ride in that jeep, either;
it looks like Jennifer's jeep,
the one we drove to Panama
City when we were eighteen
to announce the end
of the world.

So we climb into this open-air
truck instead and drink hot
beer and don't care because
who could in a place like this?
My eyes are on fire anyway,
like Plato's coming out of the
cave, so I hardly notice.

"This is our first hospital,"
she says, and adds, I think,
that it was started by a
Great Lady who's inspiring
story I don't believe because
no one really lives here and
why would heaven need a hospital?
Why?

Later we stop at the bottom
of a hill. "Our oldest military
fort is at the top, if you
want to see the ruins," and we

hike, I think, just to prove
her wrong. Cannons fired over
this water? At what? If
Aphrodite was ever born, surely
these were the waves, this was the foam.

The sun says it is time to go,
but not for me. I begin to build
a shack by the bay, walk
every morning to this wall,
and shoot at nothing.

PANAMA CITY DAWN

Can the sand be a friend?
How long until it speaks,
until the rocks cry out,
until the waves become the hand
that caresses my foot, until
the wind speaks the almost-words,
substantial only in their intentions,
the emotions that charge
the air around my ears?

It was that part of the night
when you get off the ferris wheel
and dizzily watch everyone else spin,
knowing finally that the ride
doesn't take you anywhere, really.
I walked through the house
taking stock of the eyes that
looked like mine, or at least
carried a spark that said
"Stop. Listen. Speak."

No need to do the math,
it turns out,

and so before I knew I'd left
the porch, I found myself surrounded
only by darkness,
the quiet but final *pop*
of the screen door still ringing.

I walked slowly, measuring
and recording each footfall,
Lee
taking the courthouse steps,
on to the edge of the world,
though like city limit
signs I was never sure if
I was headed in or out.

FIREFLIES

That night I spent with
hours of thoughts I
don't remember, finally
dragging the sun from
the depths by my faith
in it alone. Hoped it
would do the same for me.

And when I went to sleep
in the morning
it came easy, the hard
work over, and for once
I didn't wash off
the sand.

FATHER'S DAY

"One day I'm going
to be bigger than you,
but not for a long time,
because I'm still little,"
you say.

I'm at the sink,
washing the cake pan
from your third
birthday party,
and I feel
profundity welling up
to cover the dishes,
after-dinner philosophy
filling the soap bubbles
in expansive translucence.

But tonight,
I just smile at you,
peer out the kitchen
window into the dark,
and hand you the next
bowl to slip
into the dishwasher.

LONG AGO ONE SUMMER

Long ago one summer
I stopped my parents'
car and left them
stunned on the roadside
to roam those
sun-kissed cornfields
that grew and spread
unimpeded for miles
until I met
the farmer who
gave me a job
small wage and meals
and I worked and
worked for weeks
sweating my youth away
into the dirt I turned
while his daughter
beautiful watched and smiled
in curls from the
porch shade,
shyly.

TRESTLE

There is nothing like a train trestle
nobody uses anymore,
stately, really,
regal, almost,
despite the weeds or because
of them and
she says the things you
want to hear
and though you know they're
not true and
you can't make deals with God
it doesn't matter today
because someone is saying them
and tomorrow,
tomorrow will have to wait
because you don't know
how to get there—
but it sure isn't down
these tracks.

Sunset. And
she wants you to quit the warehouse
but you've become one
acquainted with the night
and she's not exactly the day
you met and you're not either
but as long as the train
doesn't come yet
you and she and the colors
will stay.

But it is coming,
you both hear it
in fact it's why you
keep coming back—
to insist once more
that there is no train
just tracks
and I guess that,
that is youth.

71

THE ROAD

Down here we love
the road the tracks the bridge
and I think it's because
we often have everything
we want at both ends
except hope.

Hope you find on the road
river of man snaking
into and through the woods
under a big sky.

My mother taught me hope
and love besides
on the hundreds of miles
of beat-up highway between
Ellijay and Valdosta one summer
back when the world couldn't hold me.

She never said a word

but just let me lie reclining
to stare as hard as I could
out the sunroof and into
the future straining against
my nearsightedness
at every mile marker.

Bless her for never telling me
not to look, even when she
couldn't be sure what I'd see.

And bless the road.

MODIFIED RESIDENCY

There's a spot on 25
where the land opens up
and the sky spreads out wide and grins

It hits me like revival
when I hum round that curve
and washes off all of my sins

I cry out silent inside
for unexpected blue
and the stoic grace of old fields

And when the road straightens out
and my heartbeat eases
I know I'm a man who still feels.

FLYING

You'd think that it would feel
like glory, conquest,
exultant, silver-inscribed-
platter-raising triumph,
but all I feel is small,
more than Warren's hawk
at the mortal limit only by scale,
and in the sky's vast grandeur
even that is not much, and less
special because it's science
instead of soul—It's not *me*
flying, any more than it was
me who got us to Hartsfield
in three hours.

God's got quite a view,
though, judging from what
little is visible in my little
patch of window. And if
He can see me from up
here, all my little
scratches in the earth
and self-importance,
I hope His eyes aren't
too good, or that He's
at least often distracted,
as I am now,
by the beauty of the clouds
from the other side.

MY WORDS FOR GOD

It's late July,
but at this altitude
ice crystals form on
my window and make me
think of fractals.

Past them,
I see rivers and
roads and various
other marks of man
and they make me
think of fractals.

In between,
clouds form and
air currents move
and they make me
think of fractals.

And these are my words for God.

MONTROSE

Montrose is
butterscotch drizzled
chips of chocolate
surrounding my dad's
old train set,
the one with the
little green trees
that lose a few
branches every year
but never their color.

EVERY DAY

Heaven glow and red of dawn
peeking over distant hills
lights up all that's best in us
and with a warming stillness fills.

Then, when rays are overhead,
we know that we are watched and tall;
the air is thick with destiny
and the work within us calls.

And when the glow slips down again
to kiss the earth it puts to bed,
we know we are but part of this
and destiny is in our heads.

PROCRASTINATION

I don't want to write
my autobiography,
turn myself into
something to be closed
between two great, stiff
covers and put on a shelf,
concluded and contained,
here today and hereafter.

I don't want to be a ghost yet,
and only that when someone
wants to be haunted, otherwise
dead. Most of my life dead,
past, gone. *Was*.

I want to move, change,
contradict, be something
tomorrow I wouldn't quite
recognize today: me, still,
but with a different look
in the eye, little more oak
in the voice, steadier hand.
Better somehow,
or at least more interesting,
so that if that second flap
of finality does swing around
to catch me, I'll be someone
worth putting a period after.

Until then, I'll be *out there*,
trying to live a life that
words can't hold.

DAYS SPENT

The old man said, on up-turned bucket,
Jar of jalapeños in hand:

Days spent
on porches bent
are never spent in vain.

You can log
your eighty hours
but me, I'll watch the rain.

Hours true
in eyes so blue
I'll stare and happy be.

Take off that fool necktie, boy,
and then come talk to me.

NIGHT WINDS

night winds
with iridescent fins
swimming in, swimming out.

dark grass
shows the waves rushing past
blue.

silent
like ocean-bottom sand
nothing said, nothing heard.

alone
'til you pick up the phone
blue.

ON NIGHTS LIKE THIS

on nights like this
when it looks like i
might drive right into
the moon at the top
of the next hill, when
blue and green are almost
black and the world around
me couldn't make a sound
if it wanted to, i like
to imagine myself in a kind
of God's-eye-view, a man
just driving a car on a
spinning rock (very purposefully,
of course) moving in an
elegant, mostly ignored dance
with other spinning rocks.

often i pull my foot off
the pedal. turn down the
radio. roll down the windows.
i used to even turn off
the headlights,
just for a moment,
like it might help
me slip into those
shadows between the blue
and green that are almost
black, finally free of gravity—
like if i could just be small
enough, quiet enough, listen
intently enough, i might be
part of all this enough to
hear the songs those rocks
sing as they dance,
oblivious to my presence
in a theater i pretend
to own.

I WISH

Tonight, impossibly, you asked to watch the sun set,
riding home from BLT's with your Nana and Papa,
and so, perhaps because of the strangeness of the request,
and despite the already late hour, we sat a few minutes
on the warm brick of the front steps in sinking light
and hoped for all the color the sky can hold,
the sun instead just visible in glowing orange through the
trees to the right, the moon just visible in cool blue through the
branches to the left and up. You danced in the dry grass smiling anyway,
in air hot and empty of lightning bugs, despite my straining
eyes and hopes to chase and catch them with you,
to fulfill my promise of this summer,
to catch and hold one moment worthy of the world
you deserve, the one I wish I knew how to give,
the one I wish were mine to give, the one
I wish.

HONEYSUCKLE

Honeysuckle is the day
I thought every day
would be summer,
warming me to action
perfect and free with
kisses of sun and salt,
the earth's and mine
commingled, and cooling
me only enough to be
whispered to gentle
sleep under blankets
of soft night, the last
notes of the song
of the dusk still
making the blood
in my ears dance.
And though older now
I still know I was right
then, like I know that
honeysuckle still grows,
waiting somewhere for me
with the nectar of the dusk,
waiting.

WEATHERPROOF, OR AUGUSTA SUMMER

The weatherman doesn't see
storms like these, but even he
can't miss this one—
a real show-stopper,
at least on the networks.
He will even have to find
a new radar color, maybe;
a blue so deep it bruises.

But I don't need channel six
to tell me that where I am
the rain is pounding the house
like it wants to get in,
shingles peeling, frame creaking,
but the roof holds and so
it moves, goes southpaw on me,
blow after blow on windows,
a steady stream broken only by
pointed, prodding, poking nails and
knuckles looking for cracked caulk,
and just as I start to worry
that we're back in Athens where
the rain will come up from the ground
if it must, he and I both
see that this house, *this* house
is weatherproof
and so he s l o w s,
fingers now gently tapping,
politely, a hope-I'm-not-bothering-you
caress of the panes,
a whisper:

"Come on, see how
nice it is out here?
Refreshing, even,
a change of pace,

a new perspective.
Remember?"

But I am firm, resolute.
I'm not going back.

AT THE BEACH

I don't know waves,
but they seem to know me,
and remain unimpressed.

What am I, who cannot
but wear this pale, thin
fire-brand of inexperience,
to the white, pulsing hands
that beat back and form
the edges of the world?

And why bother mentioning that they
were here before and will remain after.

We come here every year,
a pilgrimage.
Children play because they
don't know what is ahead of them,
adults because they
do know what is behind them.

I walk, periodically,
along the line,
head-down, distracted, looking away.

Sometimes I get my feet wet,
sometimes I don't, but I
almost always pull back, eventually,
from the vertigo of cliff edge.

Every now and then, though,
just for short moments,
I slip and give in
to the urge to hurl myself
at rolling Indifference.
And every time I'm surprised
when it gives.

86

BOATHOUSE

The way the branches bend and curl
makes me straight and true, and
the green filters the last light
of day just slant enough to breathe,
and the water laps against the
grass beneath the Adirondack, and
the glass sweats, and I sweat,
and the wood sweats until the
decking creaks and groans and
waits for the frosting of night
and the swing of the fan or the
breeze or both, and the music
and the water and the murmur
of voices blend with the hum of
the Earth's turn, and all of it,
all of it, is just setting for
the way your hand brushes
against mine on the boat ramp,
even the moon's soft song to the sea.

V AFTER V

V after V after V
of birds over my head
and you and me and us and we
were holding up the sun
just a little longer
spray sizzling on
technicolor clouds and
whipping wind ohmmming
beer bottles and crackers
and cheese still cold
and nowhere to go in the world
for ten more minutes and
the best night of nothing
waiting while I try to
catch the whispers of
waves but it all sounds
like "shhhh …"
and no one cares that
all the hourglasses everywhere
have spilled

RED PANTHERS

Sometimes when I close my eyes
in the sun I can smell the grass,
fresh cut and chalk-lined
under sky blue and bright,
feel the tension of cleats tied
just too tight, head full of nothing
but clear purpose, the goal material
and sure, unmistakable, only yards away
and within reach of my young legs,
friends and foes color-coded, rules
of the game agreed upon and understood,
the judges tall and solemn, absolute—
and every now and then, I'm
the hero, too, ball in the back
of the net, joyful noise enveloped,
and always, always so much time
to line up and do it again.

I LEFT FOR COLLEGE

My sister will always be
fuzzy-headed in a hot Southern
driveway, garden hose in her mouth.
Or, at my most lenient, the
Apple Princess, tiara and pink
glittering on a flatbed hay bale.

My brother, likewise, will not
age past the little blonde stinker
who never had to aim in putt-putt
or chase girls, quick with lies
so big my grandmother called them
"whoppers."

And there I am on the next page,
dashing in my blue Easter suit
under the dogwood.

So who are these people
across the table, talking
of careers and kids who
will, no doubt, soon enjoy
a good garden hose of their own?

Sometimes when it's all too much,
I crawl inside the shoebox under my
bed and bury myself under crinkled
covers, the letters they wrote when
I left for college like blankets
of deep snow.

CALLING HOME

is so hard
when it should be easy,
full instead of the terrible lack,
the coming up short, shoulders slack
from the weight of all those
things you said you'd do.

It's where the heart is, of course.
It's where you're from, who you are.
You can't forget it—
But you can't go back. Everybody knows that.

And so eventually, maybe you
buy a house and hope home materializes
out of alien ether if you just
cut the grass enough.

The funny thing?
It does. And on the best mornings it's breezy,
and slow, and light glows warm
on the old shirt that feels
just like it used to,
and home calls you instead,
just after your cereal,
and that first
cup of coffee.

VACATION BIBLE SCHOOL

I've read about manna from Heaven, sure,
but it was never real to me unless
I thought of homemade ice cream

churned by that funny machine that
almost works, watched over by the men
and their bags of ice

and served by the women in green
cafeteria mugs to be eaten
with the clanking of spoons

mingled with the sounds of horseshoes,
clapping screen doors, and weather-warped
ping-pong.

And in those brief moments between,
Where the quiet ushers in pine breezes
That mix with the vanilla trying to melt
Before you can eat it,

I understand.

SEPTEMBER—OCTOBER—NOVEMBER—DECEMBER

FIREFLIES

You can't catch lightning bugs in a jar,
not really,
or seal up fresh air in a bag.
and twilight—
well, the problem with twilight
is that we'd never know when
to stop it, if we could,
waiting always for one more
bright burst from the dying day.
In our greed we'd likely wait too long,
come away with cold heaping handfuls of night,
icy stars chilling orange to deep blue.

But of all things gold that cannot stay,
youth is surely the rarest, most ethereal.
It is everywhere, sure,
but we only see it in others,
like beauty, or happiness.
We carry it constantly for years
and complain of empty hands—
and as soon as we know we have it,
we also know it is gone.

Sometimes we even spend years,
whole lives in the worst cases,
angry that there was no sudden flash,
no tickling of the nostrils or filling of the chest,
no burning against the vast
inevitable.
Even when it aims for
The Big Moment,
some say, it does so awkwardly,
often in borrowed clothes
and poorly knotted ties.

But I do not count myself
among the worst of these,
not yet,

because even now, despite the years
and all they have brought,
sometimes scorched crimson and orange skies
bring breezes that tug at the
hairs on my neck, alerting me
to the fireflies who wait
in the corner of my eye,
still,
whispering "Come,
you haven't missed it.
It is not too late."

LOVE AND HATE

I guess you can hate words
if you love them too,
because when I can't find
the right one I feel like
my eardrums might burst
at the sound of someone,
anyone, speaking, and I
can't explain the grating,
the piercing the words cause
because then I'd have to use
them and just make it worse.

To Write: why? If it is just
going to mean loss of
soul to paper, minutes with
loved ones, work in the yard,
just for—what, exactly?
A snapshot in ink to
hold in the face of time?

Sometimes I think I would
stop if I could. But even
when I try, I can feel the
pen in my pocket, see in
my mind the corner where
the notebooks are hidden.

TEACHING AND LEARNING

The taillights pull
and I reluctantly
pledge allegiance to the
proposition that all men are created
equally capable of choosing
the right bubble to fill
the holes in our questions before
they burst and shards of
hope that can't be held
together by soap and water
scatter on cheap tile
and wait,
fodder for the push broom
of sneering, cruel
history.

A SHORT INTERVIEW ABOUT POETRY

Is your glass half-empty or half-full?

Great God! What does it matter?
What's next? *Is that a prayer*
or a curse? In the dark they're
just two sides of the same coin,
aren't they? And then what?
Rosencrantz or Guildenstern?
Heads or tails?
Answers, answers. I think
you're missing it there,
Horatio. After all,
sagacity is just articulate
guessing.

Ahem.

The glass:
Religion says God gave it to me,
Science says I made it myself.
Music wants to break it;
Philosophy doubts it's really there.
And it holds:
Hemlock? Ambrosia? Vodka? Water?
If it's not all four, I'm not
interested.
You see, there are blanks—
glorious, messy spaces to breathe, imagine—
that can't be filled in any
way that will stick.

What if I told you that
if I let go of my pen,
it might not fall,
gravity being simply expressive
of mankind's tendency toward
pessimism?

Today might be the day, you know.

DIVINE INTERVENTION

When I was sixteen
we didn't need streetlights, but we
had one, right
outside my window.
Or it seemed to be there.
Sometimes it scattered the darkness
I craved;
sometimes, late, I looked for it
and couldn't find it.
Poor maintenance, I guess.
But I *knew* it was there, still,
waiting.

Because seeing doesn't matter—
during the day it was plainly, stoicly *there*,
but at best it was an ancient sage, prosthetic limb,
eye in the middle of the hand, carved into useful
almost lifelessness,
unpredictability its last weapon.
At worst, it was one in a million
things we never see.

Because it's not the things we know,
not tragedy. It's emptiness,
the liminal space, the time between,
the waiting, that gives life
or takes it.
And that world that Zeno tried
to talk us out of—
that is the home of streetlights.

And so once, at least, years later, I know it lived—
once, at least, more than just metro envy.
I don't know who attacked and who defended,
but I couldn't take it anymore, standing
over there, hearing what I didn't tell it.
I do know that orange glow
blinded me at each *"what if ...,"*

each *"but then why ...,"*
like Jimmy Stewart's flash bulbs in *Rear Window*,
staving off the man in the shadows for another day.

Flash.

And then I think we were both tired,
and slept deeply,
like I'm sure Jacob did,
and awoke in the morning,
new.

SEPTEMBER

Tonight it was fall,
and the glass-blown earth cooled to the touch,
all shining ochres and etched pines,
and the still sky swimming pool blue and just as liquid,
birdfish trailing after the breezes of summer's last fires,
chasing whatever rays can be caught of the day ever turning,
smoothing into glassy night,
and I stand still,
and silent,
and listen intently for the soft hum
of God's finger along the rim.

MOUNTAIN LIGHT

Mountain light is different
purer somehow
and it soaks through air
that is clearer and yet
more substantial
like your first breath
was just now.

Only the leaves catch it
and toss it back and forth
while you wait
comfortably, contentedly for once,
and then it hits you
but it doesn't really
hit you it's more
like a brush from the hair
of the girl you'd die to hold
and it warms you

slow

like you should be
and then it lets you go
and all you get is
a few extra minutes
added to a life
you suddenly realize
you want to live.

RPW

Today we watched
the hawks circle
the pines and
float, my wonder
only older than
yours, until they
drifted on breezes
we couldn't feel
over the treeline
and disappeared.
You asked me where
they were going and
"at least they know"
was all I could hear
in my head.
"Maybe they'll come
back this way"
is what I said
before you ran off
to push your bubble
mower and left
me to think about
direction in case
you ask again.

A LIGHT BLANKET

Her hair reminds me that
I have always been in love
with the fall,
and my favorite split-second
of every year arrives with
that first crisp breeze, the one
scouting us out for the rest
of the season, lonely
but joyous and full of
what's to come.

I ache in August
for the expectant and hopeful
memory-dream of autumn leaves,
resplendent in their last dance
before December, burning and glowing
little flames in the grass,
the light of inspiration
against the inevitable.

I hope I, too, will one day look
sunset in the eyes, hopeful
and expectant, needing nothing
but love and a light blanket.

EYES AND HANDS AND HAIR AND SCENT

Eyes and hands and hair and scent
in autumn grass and midnight sun
on graves of battles lost and won
have caught me where the course is run
and all the temples' curtains rent.

And all the battles lost and won
on other fields in hotter day
are softened by the moonbeams' play—
and all the things we could not say
are said, and gone, and time is done.

And softened by the moonbeams' play,
all the contests fought within
though leaving scars of bite and din
are drowned with every mortal sin
by starry rustling pine trees' sway.

MEMORY

For me, it usually goes
something like this:
Open facing a street I know,
except swap that store for
the old one, the coffeeshop
for the one I haunted. Remove
various beautification efforts.

Insert me as I am, but
change the shirt, the hair,
the walk. Well, not the shirt.
Run me into faces with fuzzy
edges, listen to snippets, like
a conversation of only non sequiturs.

What is that, exactly? Convincing,
sure. Probable, even. I'd bet
there are people who, if they
saw it in a photograph, would
swear they remember that day.
The good times.

We don't make it all up, do we?

SMOKE

I worry I'm losing it—
the past I mean,
like I'm on fire and
have to watch yesterdays
twist and turn and
flutter away on the smoke,
straining to once more
catch them, re-enter
my own skin, see through
younger eyes, shift awkwardly
in the faux green leather
of that Applebee's booth,
feel the air move from the
rustle of the hem of
her white hippie shirt,
try to bring myself to
look into those eyes,
until I have to remind
myself that what matters
is that those eyes are
still blue.

WHAT IT MEANT

I used to wonder why Mister
Rogers always changed his shoes
when he came home, but now

I think it's because he had
a job, and at work he was
just that loser Fred, who

can't speak up in meetings and
packs his own lunch every morning
to eat at his desk alone. So stick

that guy in the *closet*, because
here in the neighborhood
he's a god, a benevolent puppet
master in comfortable shoes, or

at least a king, all cool calm
command in a sweater-vest robe,
and it's all castles and blue skies

as far as the mind's eye can see.
Funny how I used to think that
was a kids' show, before I knew

what it meant to be a man.

ONLY THE WIND

When the wind whips and limbs ache
to new life and sudden purpose, when
their music through melancholy sings softly,
I think often of Shelley and wonder
if translation will come, too, from the west,
or if I'm only eavesdropping on messages
not meant for me. Maybe Percy felt
the same way, fought always the secret
impulse to quietly close the windows, to
step back inside the front door for the night,
to join the chorus of mankind saying
"I thought I heard something, but it was
only the wind."

WEDNESDAY AT THE CANAL

In the October dusk
we stood looking through the railing,
all three of us, on the bridge
over the canal rushing past
parallel to the rest of the
Savannah off to our left,
always rushing away, away, away.

What is it about rivers that
makes us forever think of time?

I know I'm not the first
to get to this spot (or to fatherhood,
marriage, river-as-time metaphors)
but I don't care because the current
hits me, pulls me anyway,
and I fight the
urge to grab you both by the
hand, hold us here, now,
and wonder if my parents
ever did the same. And
their parents. (And theirs.).
Fighting the urge because
we all know that
to stop rivers is to dam(n) them.

And anyway, maybe "first"
doesn't make sense because rivers
don't really start or stop
anywhere. They just run,
while alive, fluidity
of life made physical
and fast, force made
flesh (and probably
freezing, right this minute).

But we can watch if
we want, and swim
if we dare, in its safer
swirls and eddies, bringing a little
of its essence to the land
when we leave it, dripping
its lessons from our
clothes and hair
until we get far enough
away, away, away
to forget that it
always rushes past
whether we can hear
it on the wind or not.

PASSING

Passing.
It defies you comfort, understanding,
even sadness.
The very word reminds you that
winning loses company,
progress denies place,
growth steals identity.
First *this*, now *that*.

And there are all kinds of it:
we pass time, pass tests,
pass up some lives and
pass down others.
Passing, though, no matter the type,
doesn't *fit* anywhere;
it, too, is liminal, beginning and end,
death and birth,
a doorway to a room in your house
you've never entered.
I, for one, am never sure which face
to wear with my passing clothes.

But we are supposed to be happy,
(change is good we are told)
and we should be,
for where love goes and the promise
that ours will go there too.
Nothing stays, and it couldn't,
and we shouldn't want it to, really. Still,
I can't help but notice that

For Dylan Thomas it seemed so free
to angrily cry, compose the plea—
but no such options are there for me,
who once was blind, and who now can see,

and so it makes me numb,
overwhelmed maybe,
like a system that shuts down
under the burden of too much current.

Sometimes it is the hardest thing to feel.

HICKORY FLAT

We're all trying to be
Bukowski he says let me
tell you about a movie
idea I had

and we both exhale our
lead-ballooned poetry dreams,
whiskey-soaked, into the air
between us and watch them
fall silently to sink into
the Mexican cheese dip

and in the next room they're
playing songs too good
to sing in public and doing
it too well for anybody but us
to like

and later we'll promise to
send our work to the only
people we know who'd
read it (you first)

and when it gets quiet
we'll slip out to smoke
or find a harmony nobody
wrote in the deep night blue
waiting to play the new one
nobody's heard yet

and we're all trying to be
Bukowski he says let me
tell you

THE BOX

That's what we called it,
and that's what it was,
sort of,
a large, strange cube
on Talona Mountain,
mysterious in entrance and exit.
It was probably just some abandoned
utility site, old and unneeded.

Maybe, though,
it was a mystical die thrown
by a giant, laid to rest on
that peak to remind us of
greater powers, then snatched
away when we got too familiar—
but not before I could cover
his secret runes with my own
in spray paint.

Or maybe it was a present
made by others to him and
wrapped in stone and concrete,
suiting his rough hands and heavy
touch, that he opened one night
and found empty, we having
nothing really to offer giants,
but trying anyway.

I know the truth, of course,
at least about its end:
it seems even giants are
no match for suburban sprawl,
and some nice couple from
Atlanta had it leveled
so they could erect a cottage
with a view.

Regardless, I spent my best
youth there, with a few other
wanderers, climbing
the eight-foot sides to sit
quietly and listen to the
wind when we had nothing
to say. And each of us, I think,
before we left for good, buried
someone we loved but had to
leave deep in its dark heart.

The last time I saw it,
though, was a triumphant goodbye:
I lay there on its flat top
on the coldest night of autumn
with the woman I was
starting to live for, and
watched the Old World fall
from the sky, one piece at a time,
and we counted them on their way,
so that we would not forget.

19

The day you left you said—
nothing.

Or maybe you did, but I wasn't there
and so cannot be sure if you spoke at all
or even needed to.

And then, and then, and then—
and now the miles and phone lines
do not measure distance.

I wait, but for nothing, and
I have known it.

NOVEMBER AFTERNOON

The leaves now
fall and drift and scatter
and seem to resist
the discipline and finality
of my rake
and for their sake
I should slow,
and breathe, and admit
that I would too.

HOW THE SUN LOOKS FROM MINNEAPOLIS

The great golden pearl
perched on a downy bed,
thick vapor threads of cotton
kissing candy color
coated in deep blues
voice-crack heart-break
harmonica in my head,
notes collecting cool in the corner
of my wing window,
a sweet sound for a scene of silence—
swimming pool leaves lilting, lovely, lonely.

I swear I can see the earth
curve from up here,
just a little,
icing smooth at horizon edge.
A birthday cake candle
wish to call home.

EDISTO

When we stopped in the cemetery
to change for the wedding
on the road to Edisto
the night was thick
black ink dripping from the
branches so the Spanish moss
could barely hang on,
tombstones chalky moonlight
smudges behind buildings
painted with heavy quick
strokes and all of it no more
real than the people asleep
in sketched houses nearby.
But when we dressed the stars
sang in blurred vibrations like
the reignited engine's hum,
and we slipped off the canvas
before I could get a glimpse
of the brushes in a roadside
ditch, or even wonder much
if they were dry.

ALL THESE PAGES

There are all these pages to fill
with little observations, little
insights, little revelations,
that hopefully will make
life a little richer, or
keep me the man I want to be,
so I'd better get started.

But it's silly to think that
paper will last, will be a good
defense against age, thinness,
oblivion.
It can be crumpled and tossed
with little effort; it is carried
away on light breezes.
It burns quickly in a fire.

Besides, after I finish this,
and read it over, and decide
that it's done, it might
never meet eyes again, for
even a few casual seconds.
Even mine.

But then, just the other
morning I was looking at the
buckeye my great-grandfather
gave me almost thirty years ago.
He, likely with no thought at all,
said it would be good luck.

Who knows what might last?

So, I'd better get started,
hoping my pen can hold
all the best parts of today
just in case tomorrow
might want them.
There are all these pages to fill.

WHEN ALL THE LEAVES HAVE FALLEN

What will I do when all the leaves have fallen?

I feel the season straining
against the calendar,
the great gears of the galaxy grinding,
asking always for a little more
of the time even science
now says will bend and stretch.

But will it for me?

I too burn, a red that
glows in the dusk
and dares to spend its last life,
if it must be the last,
in expansion, explosion, invasion
of space and light that
may want to be left
still and silent.

But still there is the burning,
warming, buzzing, pushing
that belies age of season—
from where and to what end
I cannot be sure, but
for something more,
fire must be.

And if it does not catch,
may my own smoke drifting
a signal be,
may I serve to soften when I fall
the ground my son is learning
to walk where he will.

STAR

You burned too bright and fell,
but the fall was truth
before the brightness.

I caught you once and for a while
tried to hold you up—
less like Atlas than
a child in the snow
transfixed by indecipherable beauty in his hands.

But you burned me too.
I thought I could take it.

And winter came on
and brilliance was cooled
by distance or time
and you've gone wherever stars go
to become whatever stars become
when they no longer burn to
beat back the night.

And we lie here, she and I,
and that world is the sky's depth
away and untouchable—
though like December night the
memory burns in time and distance
even when the life does not.

THE SNOW WILL COME

The snow will come
tomorrow,
or the next day,
Fed Ex is bringing it,
hope the tree gets
here first to
catch it,
family to watch
in the yard or
out the window,
the wind as well
to lift it, that
one delicate flake
might drift down
time and the line
I've drawn invisible
from foamy sky
to the tiny tip
of your tongue

WINTER SOLSTICE 1992

gravel and pines,
gravel and pines:
the only sounds in a
mute, still, expectant world,
those and the buzzing of stars,
like electric lights through
the holes of a blanket.

and we are children again,
and maybe we always have been,
the only difference now being
the accumulation of vast knowledge,
the work of many lifetimes, used
to hide swelled heads
and increasingly frail limbs
under spectacular forts in the basement.

that night there were just four of us,
out walking the hills while
the rest slept, or didn't exist maybe,
but we walked anyway the gravel steps of a timeless temple,
breathing like it was our first, or last,
with weight, with urgency, attentive,
a true family from one door to the next,
ducking the stars like the earth
had a ceiling we neared with each step.

and I was *lost*.
and she was *lost*.
and they were *lost*,
but none of us knew,
though we surely learned how the years
shatter young intentions like glass,
how clumsy
our first constructions are.

FIREFLIES

because at least for those minutes,
which seemed like the only minutes,
we walked the same road,
and then, as now, the pines sang;
then, as now, the gravel answered our steps;
then, as now, there was hope in those stars—
hope that was naïve then but now
knows
that whatever we build will have holes
for the stars to peek through.

HALLELUJAH

Somewhere between first Corinthians
thirteen and first John four
my arm slips toward hers
at the elbow, and hers toward
mine, divine orchestration
of celestial bodies, and in
my head I can hear the
song of my namesake, dancing
free before the Lord.

Oh, teach me, too, some melodious
sonnet—my tongue is on fire
with pentecostal promise,
but it doesn't know the words.

And when we touch:
shockwaves spread west,
volts of youth unencumbered
by wisdom or time. I have
to stifle a hallelujah.

Let there be now,
and love,
and something always
that I cannot name.

29

I want to go out, even now,
in the dark, and lie silent
in the grass, listening
to the ground whisper
in my ears. Of course,
I won't. When was the
last time I did that?
I like to think it wasn't
too long ago that I was
a small boy lying in
grass I haven't seen in
decades, praying away the
itch and those calls for
dinner so I could watch
the sky move and change
and pretend it was for me.
I swear I could feel the earth
move beneath me and
I think I knew even
then that you couldn't
stop it, that those blue
and red spots you see
when you look too long
and hard were really
moments rushing past,
daring me to catch
and hold them.
I like to think a lot
of things weren't
too long ago.

TOO MANY WORDS

I use too many words to say
what should be simple:

that love is worth it,
that skies are broad;
that time is real,
but a day is enough;
that the road is paved with pain,
but it runs through the heart of beauty.

Printed in the United States
By Bookmasters